IMAGES
of Rail

THE NORTHEAST
CORRIDOR

D1596960

"It would be difficult to overstate the importance of the Northeast Corridor to both the regional and national economies," Amtrak executive vice president and chief of Northeast Corridor (NEC) Business Development Stephen Gardner said in a January 2015 news release. "Millions of people and businesses depend on a reliable and functioning NEC and greater federal capital investment is vital to ensuring it stays that way." (Courtesy of Amtrak.)

ON THE COVER: The railroad helped develop towns and boroughs, such as Metuchen, New Jersey, into popular communities for commuters. Metuchen "is a very desirable place for suburban homes, and without question the land in this section is more favorably located than any other place between Metuchen and New York city," the *Metuchen Recorder* newspaper wrote on April 22, 1905. (Courtesy of Victor Hand Collection, Center for Railroad Photography and Art.)

IMAGES
of Rail

THE NORTHEAST CORRIDOR

Todd DeFeo

ARCADIA
PUBLISHING

Published by Arcadia Publishing
Charleston, South Carolina

Printed in the United States of America

Library of Congress Control Number: 2020935318

For all general information, please contact Arcadia Publishing:
Telephone 843-853-2070
Fax 843-853-0044
E-mail sales@arcadiapublishing.com
For customer service and orders:
Toll-Free 1-888-313-2665

Visit us on the Internet at www.arcadiapublishing.com

This book is dedicated to my lovely wife, Ruth, and to our son, Thomas. You'll be with me "Everywhere I Go."

CONTENTS

ACKNOWLEDGMENTS

For my money, there is no better place to watch trains than Metuchen, New Jersey. I am biased, I will grant you. For this is the place where I first learned of the Northeast Corridor. Of course, I did not know it as such at the time. It was just the place where I could ask conductors for expired tickets to add to my ever-growing collection and watch speeding trains blow through the station.

For a kid who loved trains, this place was magical. But let's be honest. I still find this place special. I could stand on the platform and watch trains all day long. For me, there is no place else like the Northeast Corridor for railfanning.

Thousands of commuters and through-passengers traverse these trains daily, with nary a thought about the history of this stretch of track.

For the sake of organization, this study will examine the Northeast Corridor in three sections—Boston to New York City, New York City to Philadelphia, and Philadelphia to Washington.

I am particularly appreciative of the many museums and organizations that provided me with invaluable research assistance. I am even more grateful to my wife, Ruth, for helping me develop this book, and to my parents for helping me proofread drafts to make sure it was at least somewhat coherent.

A book of this nature is not a comprehensive account of everyone associated with the railroad. Nor is it a retelling of every episode, train wreck, and corporate event related to the line. It is but a brief overview of the Northeast Corridor and its role in shaping the region and the country.

INTRODUCTION

Today, the Northeast Corridor is a highly traveled railroad line between Boston and Washington, but it was not envisioned as a high-speed railroad from the beginning. While many consider the modern incarnation as a single entity, it began as a confusing patchwork of local—and much shorter—roads.

The State of New Jersey issued the first railroad charter in the United States when it granted one to the New Jersey Railroad Company on February 6, 1815. Col. John Stevens, an inventor, lawyer, and engineer, devised the scheme.

A decade later, in 1825, Stevens built a loop of rail on his property to demonstrate the potential of railroads. His company, however, could not raise the money needed to construct its line between Camden and the Raritan River near New Brunswick and did not build any tracks. It did, however, signal the state was serious about improving its transportation network, and it laid the foundation for the Northeast Corridor.

In New Jersey, in particular, the success of the line was quickly apparent. In 1790, roughly 2,000 people traversed public roads between New York City and Philadelphia. By 1832, as railroads began operating in New Jersey, the number of people traveling between the two cities swelled to an estimated 52,000, historian J. Elfreth Watkins noted.

By 1839, the Camden & Amboy and the New Jersey Rail Road reached an agreement "by which the passenger cars will travel on the direct route from (Philadelphia) to Jersey City, thus avoiding the trouble and inconvenience of the frequent transhipments so unpleasant on the old Camden and Amboy road," the *Public Ledger* newspaper of Philadelphia reported.

It was not until about 1863 that trains operated over the entire New York–to–Washington route for the first time. However, the line at the time was far from the modern—and efficient—one the world knows today.

"We do not believe there is a railroad route in the world over which so much business is transacted, in so shameless a condition of inefficiency and discomfort as that between New-York and Washington," the *New York Times* wrote on February 6, 1863. "The distance is about 240 miles, and the time consumed in traversing it, by the fastest trains, is about twelve hours—an average of twenty miles an hour. Eight ought to be the maximum required for express trains. The cars, especially beyond Philadelphia are the very worst to be found on any important road within our knowledge," the newspaper added. "There is neither decent ventilation, respectable warmth, provision for light baggage, ordinary cleanliness, or anything else indispensable to the comfort which every passenger has a right to expect where he pays so exorbitant a fare as is demanded. The track is rough, so as to make it absolutely dangerous to travel at any high rate of speed."

Following the Civil War, on February 1, 1867, the Camden & Amboy (from New Brunswick to Trenton) and the New Jersey (from Jersey City to New Brunswick) railroads merged to form the United New Jersey Railroad and Canal Company. About this time, the Pennsylvania Railroad sought to build a connection into the nation's capital. Concurrently, in 1871, the Pennsylvania Railroad took control of the United New Jersey Railroad and Canal Company.

"The lease of the United New Jersey Railroad and Canal brought to the Pennsylvania Railroad Company very valuable property represented by shares in and bonds of branch railroads, street railroads, turnpikes, and bridges and ferries over the Delaware and Hudson Rivers," historian William Bender Wilson said.

"When the Pennsylvania Railroad Company took possession of the lines, it formed them into a grand division of its system east of Pittsburgh and Erie, and named it the United Railroads of New Jersey Division, and subdivided it into the New York and Amboy Divisions," Wilson added.

By about August 1873, the Jersey City–to–Washington trip took eight hours, a length that would be reduced over the next century. However, in the latter half of the 19th century, trains between Washington and New York City still did not enter the city. They terminated in Jersey City, New Jersey, requiring travelers to transfer to a ferry into New York City.

Arguably, the single most significant change for the corridor was the Pennsylvania Railroad's decision to build a tunnel into New York City.

With a decision to tunnel into New York City, the railroad set its plan into action. In November 1901, before making an official announcement, the Stuyvesant Real Estate Company began buying land throughout Manhattan's Tenderloin neighborhood for the site of its future station. Agents reportedly walked door to door, carrying bags of cash, to secure land from property owners. The area was a red-light district better known for corruption and prostitution than its future role as a commuter hub.

The railroad's plan did not just call for a tunnel under the Hudson River. The railroad would also build tunnels under the East River, allowing Long Island Rail Road trains to enter the station. While the plan seemed ingenious, it initially met stiff resistance from New York officials, a problem the railroad overcame.

The Boston & Providence Railroad built from Boston to Providence, Rhode Island, while three railroads—the New Haven, New London & Stonington; the New York & New Haven; and the Harlem River & Port Chester—built the majority of the line between Providence, Rhode Island, and New York City.

From New York City, the New Jersey Rail Road and Transportation Company constructed the section between Jersey City, New Jersey, and New Brunswick, New Jersey, while the Camden & Amboy Rail Road and Transportation Company laid tracks between New Brunswick, New Jersey, and Trenton, New Jersey, and the Philadelphia & Trenton Railroad forged the route between Trenton, New Jersey, and Philadelphia.

From Philadelphia, the Philadelphia, Wilmington & Baltimore Railroad constructed tracks between Philadelphia and Baltimore, and the Baltimore & Potomac Railroad built between Baltimore and Washington.

Other railroads built connection portions, and the entire Northeast Corridor eventually fell under the control of two railroads. The Pennsylvania Railroad came to control the Washington–to–New York City section of the Northeast Corridor, while the New York, New Haven & Hartford Railroad eventually came to control the portion between New York City and Boston.

To tell this story, the first four chapters of this work focus on geographic sections of the line in the early years through the early 20th century: New Jersey, the Philadelphia area, the portion from New York City to Boston, and the section between Philadelphia and Washington. The next two chapters focus on New York City's Penn Station and Washington's Union Station, while the final three chapters bring the story from the 1930s to the modern day.

One

ACROSS THE
MEADOWLANDS

On February 4, 1830, the State of New Jersey chartered the Camden & Amboy Rail Road and Transportation Company. The railroad would build a line between Camden, across the Delaware River from Philadelphia, and South Amboy, across Raritan Bay from Staten Island in New York City. By the end of 1830, workers jumped into action, and the Camden & Amboy's first horse-drawn cars operated on September 19, 1832.

Meanwhile, on March 7, 1832, the state chartered the New Jersey Rail Road and Transportation Company to build a line paralleling the Camden & Amboy. This new line would terminate at Jersey City, closer to New York City. The Camden & Amboy, worried about competition, exerted its influence in the state legislature, and the New Jersey Rail Road only built between New Brunswick and Jersey City. In turn, the Camden & Amboy would construct a new line between New Brunswick and Trenton.

To complete its line, the New Jersey Rail Road purchased or leased several companies building roads or bridges along the route, including the Newark Turnpike and bridges crossing the Passaic and Hackensack Rivers.

"Formerly the passage between Philadelphia and New York occupied from eleven to twenty hours, and was performed with great personal discomfort, and no small hazard of limb and life," New Jersey Rail Road directors wrote in 1840. "Merchandise was transported from city to city at great expense of insurance as well as of freight, and subject to all the difficulties and dangers of a coasting voyage. Now, passengers are carried from city to city during the most inclement season in from six to seven hours, and with nearly the same comfort as they enjoy at their own firesides. Merchandise is transported in less time, with less expense, and with an entire saving of insurance."

The chapter on the early years of the Northeast Corridor closed in 1871, when the Pennsylvania Railroad leased the United New Jersey Railroad and Canal Company, setting up arguably the most critical era in the line's history.

Inventor, lawyer, and engineer John Stevens, left, secured the first charter of a railroad in the United States, the New Jersey Railroad. In 1790, he successfully petitioned Congress to pass a law protecting inventors. In 1825, Stevens built a loop of rail on his property, pictured below, to demonstrate the potential of railroads. (Both, courtesy of the S.C. Williams Library, Archives and Special Collections; Samuel C. Williams Library, Stevens Institute of Technology, Hoboken, New Jersey.)

Stevens's son Robert Livingston Stevens, right, served as president of the Camden & Amboy in the 1830s and 1840s. Many credit Robert Stevens with the first all-iron rail construction. (Courtesy of the S.C. Williams Library, Archives and Special Collections; Samuel C. Williams Library, Stevens Institute of Technology, Hoboken, New Jersey.)

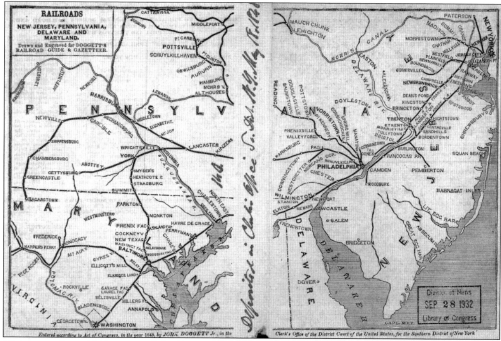

This map from 1848, created for *Doggett's Railroad Guide & Gazetteer*, shows the route of what would become the Northeast Corridor between New York City and Washington. In New Jersey, the Camden & Amboy and the New Jersey Rail Road effectively paralleled one another between the Philadelphia area and the New York City region. (Courtesy of the Library of Congress.)

Robert Stephenson and Company, a British company, built the *John Bull* locomotive for the Camden & Amboy. The railroad numbered the locomotive No. 1. It arrived in Bordentown, New Jersey, on September 4, 1831, and operated for the first time on September 15, 1831. It was also initially named *Stevens* in honor of the railroad's president, Robert L. Stevens. Below, the locomotive pulls a train out of the Pennsylvania's Jersey City terminal bound for Chicago. (Both, courtesy of the Library of Congress.)

FRANK LESLIE'S WEEKLY.

THE FAMOUS LOCOMOTIVE ENGINE, "JOHN BULL," THE FIRST EVER USED IN THIS COUNTRY, LEAVING THE PENNSYLVANIA RAILROAD-STATION IN JERSEY CITY, WITH A TRAIN OF PASSENGER-CARS, FOR CHICAGO.—DRAWN BY F. CRESSON SCHELL.

The Camden & Amboy built this 4-4-0 locomotive at the company's shops in Bordentown, a community located at the confluence of the Delaware River and two creeks (Blacks and Crosswicks Creeks). The railroad was profitable from its beginning in the early 1830s. In 1833, the railroad brought in $500,000 in gross revenue against just $287,000 in expenses. (Above, courtesy of the National Archives; below, courtesy the Library of Congress.)

One of the line's major engineering feats, the Bergen Hill Cut, was not completed when the railroad began operations. In order to start running trains, the railroad installed a temporary track around the cut. The Bergen Hill Cut opened in January 1838, ending the need for horse-drawn trains. "Several years were employed in construction before the work could be made available, though in our case, having no other competition than the stages on the old turnpikes and the steamboats by their circuitous route, we were enabled several years before the completion of our road, by the use of horse-power over Bergen Hill, to make our road partially productive," the New Jersey Rail Road and Transportation Company said in a report. (Above, courtesy of the Library of Congress; below, courtesy of Railfanning.org.)

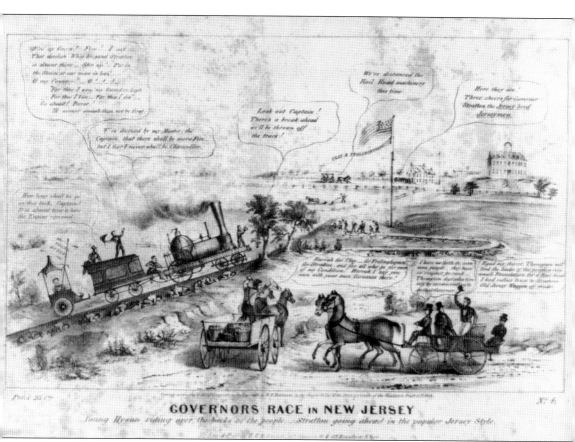

A major issue of New Jersey's 1844 gubernatorial race centered on an extension of the Camden & Amboy. Charles C. Stratton, a New Jersey native and the Whig candidate, opposed the railroad. John R. Thomson, a Pennsylvania native and the Democratic candidate, was a railroad stockholder and advocated for infrastructure improvements in the state. Stratton won with nearly 51 percent of the vote. (Courtesy of the Library of Congress.)

The United New Jersey Railroad and Canal Company was a conglomeration of the Camden & Amboy, the New Jersey Rail Road and Transportation Company, and the Delaware & Raritan Canal Company. In 1871, the Pennsylvania Railroad leased the United New Jersey Railroad and Canal Company for 999 years, setting the stage for a dramatic remaking of the line that would become the Northeast Corridor. (Courtesy of Railfanning.org.)

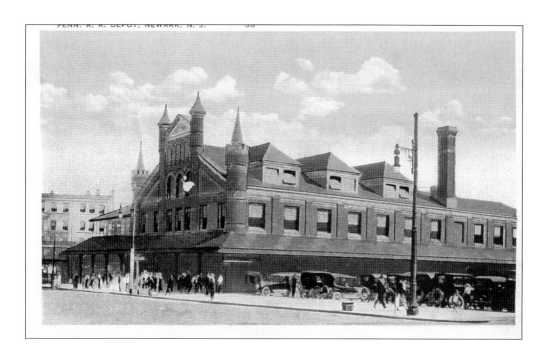

The arrival of the railroad had an immediate impact on Newark. In 1830, Newark boasted a population of about 11,000, but by 1850, the city had a population of more than 38,000. The Pennsylvania Railroad opened a new station in Newark around 1891. About two years later, the railroad elevated its tracks through the city. (Both, courtesy of Railfanning.org.)

Pennsylvania R.R. Station, Newark, N.J.

Old Railroad Station, before the Elevation, Elizabeth, N. J.

Elizabeth was an important crossing point for railroads. The New Jersey Rail Road extended its line to Elizabeth, first known as Elizabethtown, in 1835. Here, it crossed the route of the Central Railroad of New Jersey. The company, then owned by the Pennsylvania Railroad, elevated the tracks through the city between 1891 and 1894. (Both, courtesy of Railfanning.org.)

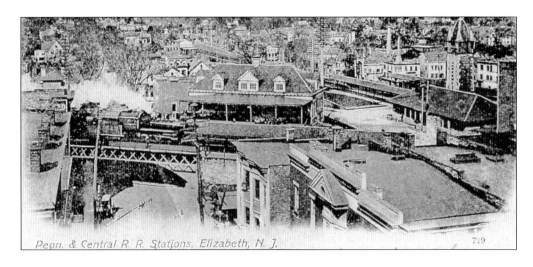

Penn. & Central R. R. Stations, Elizabeth, N. J.   729

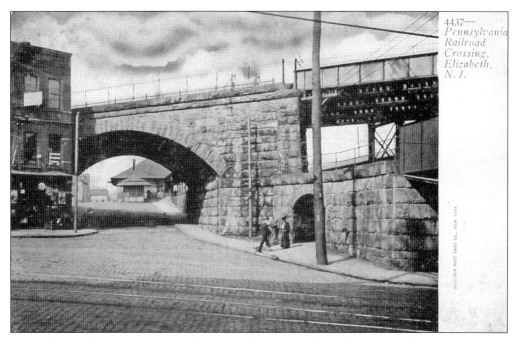

In April 1893, the first train passed over an elevated trestle in Elizabeth. "The spectators lined each side of the elevated track, and the rails were literally strewn with pennies and nickels which were placed on them by the people, who were desirous of securing souvenirs of the noteworthy event," the *New York Times* noted. "The small boys were in their element, and managed to secure a large number of the souvenir coins which were shaken off the trestle after being crushed by the car wheels. They were picked up by the urchins and sold to the persons who originally owned the coins." (Both, courtesy of Railfanning.org.)

The Pennsylvania Railroad likely opened this station in Rahway in 1885. The city has a deep history, with the earliest settlers coming to the area in the 17th century. The railroad forever changed the trajectory of the city's history. This depot stood for just three decades, and the railroad replaced it as part of a significant upgrade to the line in 1913. (Both, courtesy of Railfanning.org.)

In July 1913, the Pennsylvania Railroad opened a new $60,000 station along its newly elevated line in Rahway, pictured here in a 1920s postcard. "I recall the time when the only accommodations we had here in train service consisted of a combination baggage and passenger car seating not more than twenty-five persons," the *New York Times* quoted Rahway mayor Thomas A. Fyffe as saying during a speech to 2,500 at the station's opening. "Now the commuters have coaches for eighty persons each, and there are no more strap-hangers." (Courtesy of Railfanning.org.)

The railroad helped develop towns and boroughs, such as Metuchen, into popular communities for commuters. The postcard shows Pennsylvania Railroad's 1888 station, located at the end of the town's business district. It has been refurbished over the years but still stands. Metuchen developed into a railroad town, and at one point, several rail lines passed through the community. (Courtesy of Railfanning.org.)

The Pennsylvania Railroad broke ground on a new station in New Brunswick in October 1903, and the station formally opened in September 1904. "The new station, everyone declared to-day, is a marvel of beautiful design and finish, compared to what this city has heretofore been accustomed," the *Daily Home News* newspaper reported. "The building is said to be the finest way station on the Pennsylvania lines." (Above, courtesy of Railfanning.org; below, courtesy the Library of Congress.)

Pennsylvania R.R. Station : Western Flier at Station, Trenton, N.J. 200,388

The Camden & Amboy brought train service to Trenton in 1837 and built a wooden depot. The early-20th-century postcard above depicts the *Western Flier* train passing through Trenton. The station moved to its current location in 1863 when the railroad realigned tracks in the area. The Pennsylvania Railroad replaced the station in 1893. Successors overhauled the station in 1976 and 2008. "For a number of years trains changed engines at Trenton and New Brunswick, and not unfrequently thirty or fifty minutes were consumed in 'wooding-up' the tenders at the wood sheds along the line," historian J. Elfreth Watkins wrote. (Both, courtesy of Railfanning.org.)

TRENTON, N.J.

PENNSYLVANIA R.R. PASSENGER STATION

Trains did not always operate over the entire length of the Northeast Corridor. For example, the Pennsylvania Railroad operated the *Pennsylvania Special*, depicted in the postcard above, from Jersey City to Chicago. The train operated for the first time in June 1905 and made the trip in 18 hours. The railroad discontinued the train in November 1912 and replaced it with the *Broadway Limited*, depicted in the postcard below. (Both, courtesy of Railfanning.org.)

BROADWAY LIMITED   PENNSYLVANIA RAILROAD SYSTEM

24

Two

CONNECTING
PHILADELPHIA

While the Camden & Amboy aimed to connect New York City and Philadelphia, the railroad did not extend into either city. Instead, it required riders to transfer to a ferry to reach their destination at each end.

On the Philadelphia end of the line, a railroad connection to the city required action from the Pennsylvania General Assembly. However, the new line lawmakers chartered would not connect with the original Camden & Amboy at its terminus in Camden, but rather the terminus of its new line in Trenton.

Lawmakers chartered the Philadelphia & Trenton Railroad (P&T) on February 23, 1832, to build between its two namesake cities. The company began construction in 1833 and opened eight miles of track between Morrisville and Bristol in Pennsylvania, initially operating horse-drawn trains. The Camden & Amboy, wanting to maintain its dominance, gained a controlling stock interest in the P&T in 1836. Taking such action guaranteed the Camden & Amboy would build its line through New Brunswick and Trenton.

"By the connection of the Trenton and Philadelphia Railroad with the New Jersey Railroad, a complete line will be formed between New York and Philadelphia, capable of being traversed in 5 or 6 hours," the *United States Gazette* newspaper of Philadelphia wrote. "Not only the citizens of New Jersey, but the whole traveling public, will rejoice in the consummation of this event."

They completed a bridge over the Delaware & Raritan (D&R) Canal in 1839 in Trenton, allowing the Philadelphia & Trenton Railroad to connect with the Camden & Amboy's Trenton Branch. This bridge allowed trains to run from Philadelphia to Jersey City. However, the railroad continued to run most trains via Camden due to the location of the Philadelphia & Trenton terminal in Kensington and its proximity—or lack thereof—to the central Philadelphia business district.

To remedy the railroad's lack of connection with the city center, in 1860 the Junction Railroad formed to connect lines in and around Philadelphia, including the Pennsylvania Railroad. In 1881, the Pennsylvania Railroad took control of the Junction Railroad.

MOTHERS LOOK OUT FOR YOUR CHILDREN!
ARTISANS, MECHANICS, CITIZENS!

When you leave your family in health, must you be hurried home to mourn a

DREADFUL CASUALITY!

PHILADELPHIANS, your RIGHTS are being invaded! regardless of your interests, or the LIVES OF YOUR LITTLE ONES. THE CAMDEN AND AMBOY, with the assistance of other companies without a Charter, and in VIOLATION OF LAW, as decreed by your Courts, are laying a

LOCOMOTIVE RAIL ROAD !

Through your most Beautiful Streets, to the RUIN of your TRADE. annihilation of your RIGHTS, and regardless of your PROSPERITY and COMFORT. **Will you permit this?** or do you consent to be a

SUBURB OF NEW YORK !!

Rails are now being laid on BROAD STREET to CONNECT the TRENTON RAIL ROAD with the WILMINGTON and BALTIMORE ROAD, under the pretence of constructing a City Passenger Railway from the Navy Yard to Fairmount !!! This is done under the auspices of the CAMDEN AND AMBOY MONOPOLY !

RALLY PEOPLE in the Majesty of your Strength and forbid THIS

OUTRAGE!

Not everyone welcomed the coming of the railroad. Citizens in Philadelphia circulated this poster in 1839 to discourage the railroad's expansion. The poster, in part, claimed the Camden & Amboy and other companies were violating the law by building their railroad to Philadelphia without a charter. (Courtesy of the National Archives.)

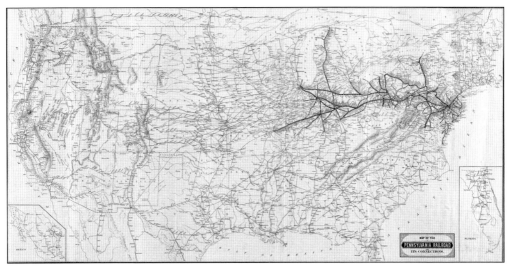

Despite its modest beginnings, by the latter half of the 19th century, the Pennsylvania Railroad grew into a dominant railroad. By 1882, the railroad was the largest company in the world, and only the federal government had a larger budget. By the end of 1926, the railroad had more than 11,640 miles of track. The railroad paid annual dividends to shareholders for more than 100 straight years. (Courtesy of the Library of Congress.)

J. Edgar Thomson led the Pennsylvania Railroad from 1852 until 1874. Under his leadership, the Pennsylvania Railroad grew exponentially, including the acquisition of the United New Jersey Railroad and Canal Company. "In all the movements which have resulted in the present enormous extension of the business of the Pennsylvania Railroad Mr. Thompson, as its president, took an active and leading part and is deserving of credit," the *New York Herald* wrote in Thompson's May 1874 obituary. (Courtesy of the Library of Congress.)

The Commonwealth of Pennsylvania chartered the Pennsylvania Railroad in 1846. In the 1860s and 1870s, the railroad grew significantly, including the 1871 acquisition of the United New Jersey Railroad and Canal Company, which gave the railroad access to the doorstep of New York City. It spent the better part of the next four decades building a direct route into the city. (Both, courtesy of the Library of Congress.)

PENNSYLVANIA RAILROAD.

THE GREAT TRUNK LINE,
AND
MOST DIRECT ROUTE TO THE
WEST, NORTHWEST, AND SOUTHWEST.

Pullman Palace Cars are run to Chicago, Cincinnati, Louisville, Indianapolis, and St. Louis, without change.

SPEED, COMFORT, AND SAFETY GUARANTEED BY

Steel Rails, Iron Bridges, Stone Ballast, Double Track, Westinghouse Air Brakes, and the
MOST IMPROVED EQUIPMENT.

Tickets Sold, and Information given in regard to Trains, etc., at the Offices of the Company.

PHILADELPHIA.
S. E. Corner BROAD and CHESTNUT STS., No. 631 CHESTNUT ST., No. 116 MARKET ST., No. 4000 MAIN STREET, GERMANTOWN, DEPOT, 32d and MARKET STS.

NEW YORK.
No. 526 BROADWAY, No. 435 BROADWAY, No. 271 BROADWAY, No. 1 ASTOR HOUSE, No. 944 BROADWAY, No. 8 BATTERY PLACE, DEPOT, Foot of DESBROSSES STREET, DEPOT, Foot of CORTLANDT STREET.

BOSTON.
Nos. 17 and 19 WASHINGTON STREET.

BALTIMORE.
N. E. Corner BALTIMORE and CALVERT STREETS, CALVERT STATION, N. C. R. R.

WASHINGTON.
N. E. Corner THIRTEENTH STREET and PENNSYLVANIA AVENUE, N. E. Corner SIXTH STREET and PENNSYLVANIA AVENUE, DEPOT, BALTIMORE AND POTOMAC RAILROAD, Corner SIXTH and B STREETS.

PITTSBURG.
UNION DEPOT, No. 18 FIFTH AVENUE.

Principal Ticket Offices in New England, Eastern Pennsylvania, and at all Hotel Ticket Offices.

A. J. CASSATT.
Gen'l Manager.

D. M. BOYD, Jr.,
Gen'l Pass. Agent.

The Pennsylvania Railroad ran this advertisement around 1874, which promoted the railroad's safety thanks to double-tracked lines, stone ballast, Westinghouse air brakes, and other features. (Courtesy of the Library of Congress.)

The Pennsylvania Railroad built a stone bridge spanning the Delaware River between 1901 and 1903, ending the need for trackage rights over another bridge. (Courtesy of Railfanning.org.)

The Pennsylvania Railroad completed the stone arch bridge over the Delaware River in 1903. The bridge is one of the largest the Pennsylvania ever built. To cross the river, Philadelphia & Trenton initially acquired the Trenton Delaware Bridge Company and constructed tracks on the company's wooden toll bridge, originally erected in 1806. The railroad initially ran horse-drawn trains over the bridge. In 1835, the railroad reinforced the bridge to support steam locomotive operations. (Both, courtesy of the Library of Congress.)

6. N.Y. CONNECTING BRIDGE, PHILADA.

The Pennsylvania Railroad subsidiary, the Connecting Railway, founded in 1863, built a 6.75-mile-long line connecting the Philadelphia & Trenton and the Pennsylvania railroads in Philadelphia. In the city, the railroad built an impressive bridge across the Schuylkill River. The bridge was completed by 1867 and significantly overhauled in 1915 to accommodate increased volumes of traffic passing over the line in the early 20th century. (Courtesy of the New York Public Library.)

The Pennsylvania Railroad opened Broad Street Station in 1881, bringing its passenger trains into the heart of Philadelphia. To accommodate its trains, the railroad built a massive train shed in 1892, pictured below. The shed had the largest roof span in the world. The railroad demolished the shed following a fire in 1923, but the railroad continued to use the station until 1952. It was demolished the following year. (Both, courtesy of the Library of Congress.)

Philadelphia architect Theophilus P. Chandler designed the Pennsylvania Railroad station in North Philadelphia. This station opened in 1901 to replace a smaller one dating to the 1870s. The railroad expanded the station between 1912 and 1915. In 1991, Amtrak built a new station to replace the 1901 building, which was subsequently renovated as commercial space. (Both, courtesy of the Library of Congress.)

The Pennsylvania Railroad began construction on the Thirtieth Street Station in 1927 to replace its station in West Philadelphia. The station opened in March 1933, even though it was only partially completed. Chicago architectural firm Graham, Anderson, Probst & White designed the Classical Revival building, which sits on the west bank of the Schuylkill River. When it opened, the station was home to several technological innovations, including an elaborate intercom system. (Both, courtesy of the Library of Congress.)

Zoo Junction, located near the Philadelphia Zoo, hence its name, and pictured here in 1977, is the junction of the Northeast Corridor and Keystone Corridor in Philadelphia. The Keystone Corridor runs between Philadelphia and Harrisburg. (Courtesy of the Library of Congress.)

Three

NORTHWARD TO BOSTON

The line that would become the Northeast Corridor between New York City and Boston, the eventual northern terminus of the line, was just as fractured as its southern counterparts.

In 1834, the railroad opened a segment between Boston and Canton, Massachusetts. Another section opened in 1835 after workers finished the Canton Viaduct in Canton.

Meanwhile, the New York & Stonington Railroad chartered in Connecticut in May 1832, and the New York, Providence & Boston Railroad chartered in Rhode Island in June 1832. On July 1, 1833, they joined to create the New York, Providence & Boston Railroad, often called the Stonington Line.

On November 17, 1837, the New York, Providence & Boston Railroad opened a 50-mile line between South Providence, Rhode Island, and Stonington, Connecticut. In Stonington, passengers could take a steamboat to New York City, traveling through the Long Island Sound. In Providence, travelers could take a car float across the Providence River to India Point, where they could continue on the Boston & Providence Railroad.

In 1888, the Old Colony Railroad, formed initially to connect Boston and Plymouth, Massachusetts, acquired the Boston & Providence, while in 1893, the New York, New Haven & Hartford Railroad gained control of the Old Colony Railroad.

In his inaugural address in January 1896, Boston mayor Josiah Quincy called for a new station to serve as a terminus for all railroads entering the city from the south. "The business interests of Boston, in my opinion, would be as greatly benefited by some such union of terminals and concentration of freight and passenger business on the part of the four railroads entering the city on the south side."

On New Year's Day 1899, the Boston Terminal Company, a company chartered in 1876 and comprised of several railroads, including the Boston & Providence and the New York, New Haven & Hartford, opened Boston's South Station. The five-story Neoclassical Revival–style station today marks the northern terminus of the Northeast Corridor.

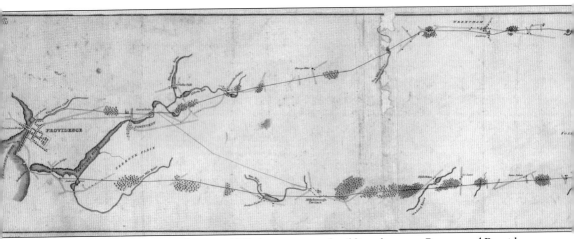

This topographic strip map dating to 1828 shows proposed rail lines between Boston and Providence. In January 1828, the Board of Internal Improvement presented to Massachusetts governor Levi

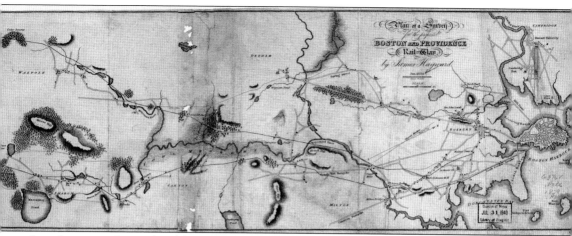

Lincoln a report for a railroad from Boston to Providence. The board recommended horse-powered trains operate over a single set of tracks. (Courtesy of the Library of Congress.)

The Boston & Providence Railroad used the above station in Park Square in Downtown Boston. A newer terminal, below, opened around 1874. That terminal closed when the newer South Station opened in 1899; though, it was not demolished until about 1905. (Both, courtesy of the New York Public Library.)

40

The opening of Boston's South Station in 1899 "will raise to a distinctly higher level the impression which Boston will hereafter make upon the traveler who visits our city, to compare it with others; for he will here find one of the very finest examples of a great passenger terminal to be found anywhere in the world, and the impression will be created upon his mind from the moment of his arrival that it must be no mean city which receives the stranger in such ample and dignified surroundings," Mayor Josiah Quincy said, according to the *Boston Daily Globe*. (Both, courtesy of the Library of Congress.)

Back Bay Station was built at the crossing of the Boston & Providence and Boston & Albany railroads. In 1899, the railroads built the station, pictured above in a c. 1910 postcard, but it burned in 1928. A replacement station, pictured below in 1979, opened the next year, but a newer Back Bay Station replaced it in 1987. (Above, courtesy of Railfanning.org; below, courtesy of the Library of Congress.)

The Boston & Providence Railroad built the Canton Viaduct in 1834–1835 in Canton, Massachusetts. Upon its completion, it was the longest and tallest railroad viaduct in the world and is said to be the last-surviving viaduct of its kind. The viaduct "is a splendid work, which might in the days of yore, have done honor to the enterprise of an Emperor. But now, private efforts accomplish such things without parade," the *Journal of Commerce* reported at the time. (Both, courtesy of the Library of Congress.)

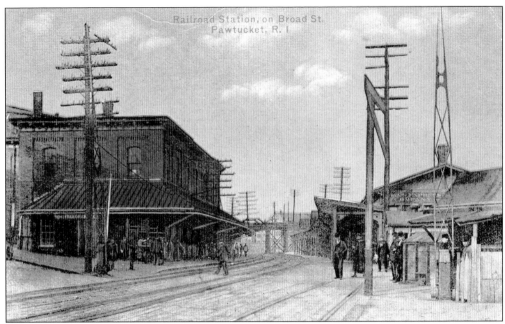

The New York, New Haven & Hartford Railroad built a new Pawtucket–Central Falls station in 1915–1916 to replace separate stations in Pawtucket, pictured above, and Central Falls. The house station above the tracks, pictured below in 1977, closed in 1959, but trains continued to stop at the station's platforms until 1981. The station remains in place, straddling the Northeast Corridor. (Above, courtesy of Railfanning.org; below, courtesy of the Library of Congress.)

The first station in Providence opened in 1847 but was soon too small for the volume of traffic passing through the city. It burned down in February 1896, and a new Union Station, pictured below, was built between 1896 and 1898. Another new, smaller station opened in 1986, and the former Union Station was refurbished as a mixed-use destination. (Above, courtesy of Railfanning. org; below, courtesy of the Library of Congress.)

1176- Providence, R. I.
"Bay State Limited" in Union Station.

A postcard from around 1918 depicts the *Bay State Limited* train in Providence, Rhode Island. The New York, New Haven & Hartford Railroad operated the train between New York and Boston. The train made its first run on June 26, 1893. (Courtesy of Railfanning.org.)

The New York, New Haven & Hartford Railroad and the New London Northern Railroad teamed up to build the New London, Connecticut, station to replace an earlier depot destroyed by fire in 1885. Boston architect Henry Hobson Richardson designed the station, which opened in 1887 and sits along the Thames River. (Courtesy of the Library of Congress.)

The New London Station was nearly demolished in the 1960s, prompting a fight between local residents who wanted to save the structure and a local redevelopment authority that wanted to raze the structure and redevelop the site. In 1971, the station was added to the National Register of Historic Places. Following negotiations, Union Station Associates purchased the station in 1975, saving it from demolition. (Both, courtesy of the Library of Congress.)

Old Saybrook, Connecticut, was an important railroad junction for the New York, New Haven & Hartford and the Connecticut Valley railroads. The New Haven constructed a depot here in 1873, a building both railroads shared. In 2002, Amtrak rebuilt the station as part of a $2.6 million project. The former freight building was converted into a restaurant space. (Both, courtesy of the Library of Congress.)

Connecting the line with New York City and New England required a bridge across the East River. The Hell Gate Bridge opened in 1917. "The long cherished dream of railroad men to link New England by an all rail route via New York city with states lying west and south of the Hudson and East rivers is realized," the *Daily Home News* reported at the time. German spies targeted the bridge as part of the failed Operation Pastorius during World War II. (Both, courtesy of the Library of Congress.)

Four

SOUTHWARD TO WASHINGTON

South of Philadelphia, the Philadelphia, Wilmington & Baltimore Railroad was the dominant railroad responsible for building the line that became the Northeast Corridor.

The railroad was created through the merger of four earlier railroads: the Philadelphia & Delaware County, the Baltimore & Port Deposit, the Delaware & Maryland, and the Wilmington & Susquehanna. The new line formed a single road between Philadelphia and Baltimore. The Pennsylvania Railroad took control of the company in 1881.

"An important constituent of a great North and South line of transportation, it challenges ocean competition, and carries on its rails not only statesmen and tourists, but a valuable interchange of products between different lines of latitude," historian William Bender Wilson wrote of the line in his 1895 history of the Pennsylvania Railroad. "As a military highway, it is of the greatest strategic importance to the national, industrial, and commercial capitals—Washington, Philadelphia and New York. It presents some of the very best transportation facilities to the commerce of the cities after which it is named, and could not be obliterated from the railroad map of the United States without materially disturbing its harmony."

At Baltimore, the Baltimore & Ohio Railroad initially completed the line to Washington. To continue its southward push, the Pennsylvania secured the charter of the Baltimore & Potomac, chartered initially in the 1850s. The Pennsylvania instead pushed the line to Washington, and it opened on July 2, 1872.

A few years earlier, in 1861, the Pennsylvania Railroad gained control of another railroad, the Northern Central Railway, which ran from Baltimore to the Susquehanna River, giving it access into Baltimore.

In 1871, the railroad bored the 7,669-foot-long Baltimore and Potomac Tunnel beneath the city of Baltimore. Even though the rest of the line opened in 1872, the railroad did not complete the tunnel until 1873. Union Railroad completed a second tunnel, the Union Tunnel, leading to Union Station (later Pennsylvania Station) in Baltimore.

In 1902, the Pennsylvania Railroad merged the Philadelphia, Wilmington & Baltimore and the Baltimore & Potomac railroads to create the Philadelphia, Baltimore & Washington Railroad.

The old P. B. W. R. R. Station, Front and French Streets, Wilmington, Del.

GEORGE A. WOLF, WILMINGTON, DEL.

In the early years of the 20th century, the Pennsylvania Railroad decided to elevate its tracks through Wilmington, similar to work performed in New Jersey. In 1901, the railroad announced plans for the massive project, which necessitated a new station to replace an earlier one the Philadelphia, Wilmington & Baltimore built. Construction on the elevation is pictured below. (Both, courtesy of the Library of Congress.)

PENNSYLVANIA IMPROVEMENTS AT WILMINGTON—TOP OF BRICK ARCHES FROM CROSSINGS NORTHWARD.

PENNSYLVANIA IMPROVEMENTS AT WILMINGTON—B. & O. AND P. & R. CROSSING

Chief engineer William H. Brown developed the pass for the viaduct through Wilmington. Elevating the tracks accomplished two goals for the railroad. It straightened the line, and it also eliminated several grade crossings. "When the improvements are completed they will probably result in the saving of several minutes in the running time between Philadelphia and Baltimore—marking another step in the accomplishment of the purpose of the Pennsylvania Railroad eventually to reduce its running time between New York and Washington to four hours," the *Railway Age* wrote in 1907. (Both, courtesy of the Library of Congress.)

Wilmington was the headquarters of the Pennsylvania Railroad's Philadelphia, Wilmington & Baltimore subsidiary. The Pennsylvania Railroad elevated its tracks through Wilmington between 1902 and 1908. Furness, Evans, and Company designed a new station for the railroad, which opened around 1908, replacing an earlier station the Philadelphia, Wilmington & Baltimore Railroad constructed. In 2011, the station was renamed for former vice president Joe Biden. (Both, courtesy of the Library of Congress.)

THE P. B. & W. RAILROAD DEPOT, FRONT AND FRENCH STS., WILMINGTON, DEL.

The Philadelphia, Baltimore & Washington Railroad built the Wilmington Shops in Wilmington, Delaware, around the turn of the 20th century. The new facility replaced shops built half a century earlier. The facility included a roundhouse and a paint shop. Today, the shops, as pictured in April 1977, are the primary facility for the repair and overhaul of electric locomotives on the Northeast Corridor. (Both, courtesy of the Library of Congress.)

"The whole plant, from the general lay-out to the location and power of individual machine tools, is the result of careful design extending over a comparatively long period," the *Railway Age* wrote in 1904. In the photograph below, GG-1 locomotives and a Swedish electric locomotive Amtrak tested as part of its process to find a replacement for the GG-1 are among those in the shop for service. (Both, courtesy of the Library of Congress.)

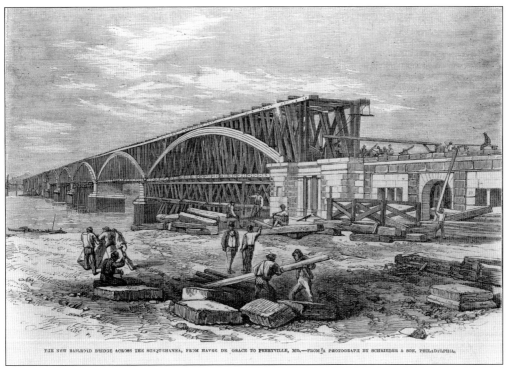

THE NEW RAILROAD BRIDGE ACROSS THE SUSQUEHANNA, FROM HAVRE DE GRACE TO PERRYVILLE, MD.—FROM A PHOTOGRAPH BY SCHREIBER & SON, PHILADELPHIA.

The Philadelphia, Wilmington & Baltimore Railroad relied on a ferry service to transport passengers across the Susquehanna River starting in 1838. The railroad completed a wooden bridge across the river in 1866. The Pennsylvania Railroad replaced the bridge, building a more formidable structure in 1904–1906. The original bridge was converted for use as a vehicle crossing but was dismantled during World War II. (Both, courtesy of the Library of Congress.)

PASSENGER AND FREIGHT STATIONS, PRESIDENT STREET, BALTIMORE.

The Philadelphia, Wilmington & Baltimore's Greek Revival President Street Station in Baltimore, pictured above, opened in 1850. On April 19, 1861, the station was the backdrop of the Pratt Street Riots, also known as the Pratt Street Massacre. The fight pitted antiwar Copperhead Democrats and Confederate sympathizers against state militia regiments from Massachusetts and Pennsylvania heading to Washington for service. The riot saw some of the first deaths of the Civil War, earning the fight the nickname of the "First Bloodshed of the Civil War." Elsewhere, the railroad was the scene of bloody fighting during the Civil War, pictured below. (Both, courtesy of the Library of Congress.)

THE INVASION OF MARYLAND—CAPTURE OF A TRAIN ON THE PHILADELPHIA, WILMINGTON AND BALTIMORE RAILROAD AT MAGNOLIA, NEAR GUNPOWDER RIDGE, JULY 11.—FROM A SKETCH BY OUR SPECIAL ARTIST.—SEE PAGE 295.

After a new Union Station opened in Baltimore in 1873, the Pennsylvania Railroad converted President Street Station into a freight-only depot. By the 1970s, the train sheds were severely deteriorated, and a series of fires destroyed them. Today, only the headhouse (station building) remains. (Both, courtesy of the Library of Congress.)

The Northern Central Railway used the Calvert Station, also called Calvert Street Station, in Baltimore beginning in 1850. In 1861, the Pennsylvania Railroad gained a controlling interest in the line, giving it access to Baltimore as it continued to expand toward Washington. After Baltimore's Union Station opened, the station was redundant, but the railroad continued to use it. It was razed in 1949. (Both, courtesy of the Library of Congress.)

New York architect Kenneth Murchison designed Baltimore Pennsylvania Station, originally known as Union Station. The railroad opened the Beaux-Arts Classical-style depot in 1911 in the geographic center of Baltimore. It sits on the site of earlier stations, including Northern Central Railway's Union Station, completed in 1873 and expanded in 1880s. (Both, courtesy of the Library of Congress.)

The Baltimore & Potomac Railroad opened its station in Washington in July 1872. The depot was the scene of the July 2, 1881, shooting of Pres. James A. Garfield. Charles J. Guiteau shot Garfield as he was waiting to board a train for New Jersey, where he would take his summer vacation. The Pennsylvania Railroad closed the station in 1907, moving its operations to Union Station. (Both, courtesy of the Library of Congress.)

Five

BUILDING TO
NEW YORK CITY

In December 1901, Alexander Cassatt, president of the Pennsylvania Railroad, announced a bold plan to build a tunnel beneath the North River (Hudson River). It would allow the railroad to accomplish a long-standing goal to run its trains into the city.

In conjunction with the tunnel, the railroad announced plans to build a massive new station in the heart of Manhattan. The railroad acquired property for the station, simply named Pennsylvania Station.

Pennsylvania Railroad officials had long discussed building a line into the city. The railroad could either build a bridge or dig a tunnel. A tunnel posed many problems. One was steam locomotives could not use the tunnel, and following a deadly wreck, the New York Legislature banned steam locomotives in Manhattan starting July 1, 1908. Another was the feasibility of construction. An industrialist named DeWitt Clinton Haskins tried to tunnel beneath the Hudson River beginning in 1879, but he abandoned the project after a decade of work, which included several blowouts.

The Pennsylvania Railroad hired engineer Gustav Lindenthal to design a bridge across the river. In 1890, Lindenthal secured a federal charter to build the bridge. However, plans for a massive bridge across the river failed by 1900 or 1901 when other railroads balked at sharing the cost of construction, leaving the railroad to go it alone. While Lindenthal did not build the railroad bridge across the Hudson, he did design others in the New York City region.

In the summer of 1901, Cassatt traveled to Europe for vacation. While in Paris, Samuel Rea, then a vice president of the railroad, urged Cassatt to explore the new Gare d'Orsay train station before leaving the city. Cassatt spent a significant amount of time studying how the railroad used electric trains to travel in and out of the station. His observation cemented the plan—the Pennsylvania Railroad would build a tunnel under the Hudson River to bring its trains into New York City.

A 2052   Entrance to Penn. R. R. Ferry, Jersey City, N. J.

This is pretty close to New York. Just over the river. Norman

The earliest incarnation of Pennsylvania Railroad's Exchange Place Station in Jersey City, the then terminus of its rail line, opened in 1834. Here, passengers heading to New York City transferred to a ferry to points in Manhattan, including Thirty-fourth Street or Cortland Street. The railroad replaced the terminal in 1876 and again starting in 1888. (Both, courtesy of Railfanning.org.)

PENNSYLVANIA FERRIES, JERSEY CITY, N. J.

The original *New Brunswick* ferry was built in 1866 and ran between New Jersey and New York City. In 1889, the *New Brunswick* burned, but the railroad rebuilt it as a double-decker. On December 28, 1896, it burned a second time and was a total loss. The replacement *New Brunswick* is pictured above around 1905. (Courtesy of the Library of Congress.)

The Pennsylvania Railroad's *Annex 5* ferry passes Battery Park in Lower Manhattan. On March 31, 1897, it burned, with the fire "furnishing a brilliant spectacle for the entertainment of passengers on the various ferryboats in her neighborhood and an object of interest to many persons in upper stories of high buildings in the lower portion of" New York City, the *New York Times* reported. (Courtesy of the Library of Congress.)

In the photograph above, people and carts loaded with goods appear at the offices for the Pennsylvania and the Camden & Amboy railroads, at Pier No. 1 in New York City, around 1865. Below is a view from the Washington Building, near Battery Park, looking west across the North River (Hudson River) and Bay toward Jersey City. The Pennsylvania Railroad Pier is in the foreground. (Both, courtesy of the Library of Congress.)

The Pennsylvania Railroad opened its new Twenty-third Street ferry terminal in Manhattan in 1897. Of the complex, pictured between 1900 and 1915, the *World* newspaper of New York City remarked, "Among the many advantages and conveniences of which Greater New York comes into immediate possession and which will be instrumental in her still greater development there are few which deserve more consideration than the new Twenty-third Street ferry." (Courtesy of the Library of Congress.)

Samuel Rea first joined the Pennsylvania Railroad in 1871. One of his most significant accomplishments may be helping to bring the railroad into New York City. On January 1, 1907, Rea laid the cornerstone of the new station at the corner of Seventh Avenue and Thirty-third Street. On March 1, 1909, the railroad officially named its new Manhattan station Pennsylvania Station. The station opened in 1910, serving both the Long Island and the Pennsylvania railroads. Rea went on to serve as the Pennsylvania Railroad's ninth president from 1913 to 1925. (Courtesy of the Library of Congress.)

DAVIS & SANFORD

· FIFTH AVENUE · NEW YORK ·

Alexander J. Cassatt served as the seventh president of the Pennsylvania Railroad from 1899 to 1906. He joined the railroad in 1861, initially as an engineer, and rose through the company's ranks. Although he was president of the railroad for only a few years, his impact was tremendous. (Courtesy of the Library of Congress.)

As the Pennsylvania Railroad built Penn Station, the railroad helped spawn a new industry—public relations—when it hired Ivy Lee, pictured above, and George F. Parker to help change its public perception. "The Pennsylvania Railroad thus recognizes the value of having the news of this great enterprise put accurately before the public," the *Wall Street Journal* reported on July 23, 1906. "This is a new departure on the part of this railroad." (Courtesy of the Library of Congress.)

The Pennsylvania Railroad explored both tunnels and a bridge to cross the Hudson River for direct access into Manhattan. A group of designers under the leadership of chief engineer Charles M. Jacobs began their work on the tunnels in 1902; the original plan called for three tubes, later revised to two. (Above, courtesy of the Library of Congress; below, courtesy of Railfanning.org.)

Interior of Pennsylvania Tunnels, New York.

The Pennsylvania Railroad tunneled beneath the Hudson River between 1904 and 1908. The tunnels connecting Weehawken, New Jersey, and Manhattan allowed its trains to reach the city directly. "After years of exhaustive study the conclusion has been reached that a tunnel line operated by electricity is in every way the most practical, economical and the best both for the interests of the railroad company and of the city," the *New York Tribune* quoted Cassatt as saying. The railroad formally opened the tunnels on November 27, 1910, along with the new Pennsylvania Station, known colloquially as Penn Station. (Both, courtesy of Railfanning.org.)

Work on Pennsylvania Station began in 1904, and workers would eventually raze roughly 500 buildings covering a 28-acre swath of land in the heart of Manhattan to construct the massive new station. Work was not without dangers. In June 1906, two workers died following a massive accident in the tunnel, which sent a geyser of muck reaching a height of 40 feet out of the river. Word of the disaster made headlines in newspapers, prompting many safety concerns. (Both, courtesy of the Library of Congress.)

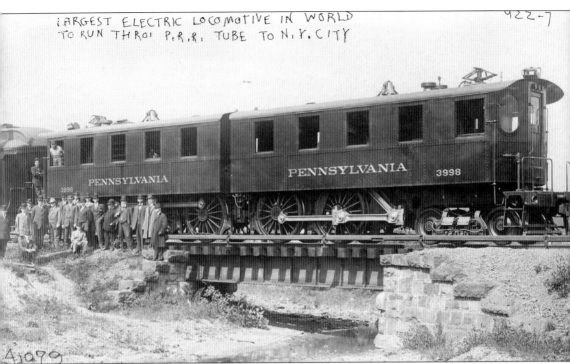

Steam trains were banned from operating into Pennsylvania Station. Instead, electric locomotives replaced steam locomotives to pull trains into the city at Manhattan Transfer. The Pennsylvania Railroad had to develop a new electric locomotive, the DD1. The railroad built a total of 66 DD1 locomotives (33 married pairs) at its Altoona Works complex in Altoona, Pennsylvania. (Courtesy of the Library of Congress.)

National Park Service photographer Jack E. Boucher took this photograph in April 1977 of the Hudson River tunnel for the Historic American Engineering Record. While the Northeast Corridor has four or six tracks for much of its route through New Jersey, the line reduces to two tracks before the tunnels to Manhattan—one for each tube beneath the river—a source for bottlenecks. (Courtesy of the Library of Congress.)

The Pennsylvania Railroad began using the new station in November 1910, a few months after the Long Island Rail Road started using the edifice. "As the crowd passed through the doors into the vast concourse on every hand were heard exclamations of wonder for none had any idea of the architectural beauty of the new structure," the *New York Times* reported. "From end to end the station was ablaze with lights." (Both, courtesy of the Library of Congress.)

"The completion of the work signalizes the success of the greatest corporate undertaking of any period," the Pennsylvania Railroad wrote of the project in a promotional piece from 1910. "In the amount of money involved and the scope of the work with all its correlated parts, the achievement is second only to the building of the Panama Canal, an enterprise backed by the wealth of the nation and prosecuted under national control." (Both, courtesy of the Library of Congress.)

"When the two tracks emerge from the tubes under the Hudson and reach the entrance to the station yards at Tenth Avenue they begin to multiply, and at Ninth Avenue, and extending into the station, the number has grown from two to twenty-one," the railroad wrote of the station in a 1910 promotional piece. "The location of the station appeals directly to the hotel guest, the shopper, the amusement seeker, the business man, the professional man, and every class of travelers to and from New York over the Pennsylvania Railroad." (Both, courtesy of Victor Hand Collection, Center for Railroad Photography and Art.)

The famed Pennsylvania Station in Manhattan was noted for its glass dome. The architects drew inspiration from the Gare d'Orsay in Paris, which today is no longer a railroad station and is home to one of the world's best art museums. "The terminal itself is a monument to the ingenuity of the present day architects and engineers," the *Asbury Park Evening Press* reported in September 1910. "It is provided with every known convenience for the passenger." (Both, courtesy of Victor Hand Collection, Center for Railroad Photography and Art.)

While the original Penn Station was noted for the amount of light allowed to illuminate the track level, the modern incarnation of the station is known for its dark, basement-like atmosphere. To many, the current station is a confusing maze of subterranean tunnels. "One entered the city like a god," architectural historian Vincent Scully famously wrote. "One scuttles in now like a rat." (Above, courtesy of the Library of Congress; below, photograph by the author, courtesy of Railfanning.org.)

A power outage in August 2003 left much of the Northeast in the dark, and the outage rendered the departures board in Penn Station useless. Despite the outage, Amtrak and New Jersey Transit still managed to operate trains on the Northeast Corridor and into Penn Station on a reduced schedule. (Photograph by the author; courtesy of Railfanning.org.)

While the modern incarnation of Penn Station is a shell of its former self, there are some remnants to remind travelers and the public alike of its former splendor. Outside the station stands a pair of eagles, one pictured here in 2019, that once stood atop the original structure. A statue of Samuel Rea, a former vice president and president of the Pennsylvania Railroad, is also on display outside the station. (Photograph by the author; courtesy of Railfanning.org.)

Six

WASHINGTON'S UNION STATION

By the turn of the 20th century, the dominant railroads serving the nation's capital had separate stations. When city leaders in Washington wanted to beautify the city, one of the major initiatives was a new train station.

So, in 1901, the Baltimore & Ohio and the Pennsylvania railroads announced plans to build a new joint station. The US Senate Park Commission tapped Daniel Burnham, a well-known architect, to orchestrate a comprehensive beautification plan for the nation's capital. The idea was to make it a fitting entrance to the city.

For inspiration, Burnham turned to Maj. Peter Charles L'Enfant, a French American military engineer who was a contemporary of George Washington during the Revolutionary War and who developed the plan for the city of Washington. L'Enfant's work helped establish the National Mall.

Burnham's plan included a new Union Station for the district, one that removed the rail lines from the center of the mall. The station, owned by the Washington Terminal Company, a company jointly owned by the Baltimore & Ohio Railroad and the Philadelphia, Baltimore & Washington Railroad, opened on October 27, 1907. However, workers did not complete the edifice until April 1908. The Pennsylvania Railroad moved its operations into the station on November 17, 1907.

The Northeast Corridor was the scene of some dramatic mishaps, but perhaps none was more famous than when a train fell through the floor at Washington's Union Station. In January 1953, the station was the site of a crash involving the *Federal Express* passenger train from Boston. The GG-1 locomotive overran the platform and smashed through a barrier; the weight of the train caused the floor to collapse. Miraculously, no one was killed in the crash.

By 1967, as railroad traffic struggled, a commission recommended Union Station serve as a visitors' center during the upcoming bicentennial celebration. The concept ultimately passed, and the visitors' center opened on July 4, 1976.

However, by the 1980s, Union Station was in poor condition. In 1981, the National Park Service declared the building unsafe and ordered it closed after a portion of the station's ceiling collapsed in the wake of heavy rain.

Union Station remained closed for a significant refurbishment project under the Union Station Redevelopment Act of 1981. In 1983, the federal Department of Transportation established the Union Station Redevelopment Corporation to help with Union Station's restoration. The current iteration of the station opened on September 29, 1988.

"What the new station will be when completed can be seen by the most casual observer," the *Washington Times*, a different newspaper from the current publication that shares its name, noted in its October 27, 1907, edition. "A thing of beauty, composed of magnificent arches and wonderful distances, it will also provide every known facility in modern transportation." (Both, courtesy of the Library of Congress.)

"The building of this great terminal was made possible by the cooperation of the government with the railways, with the intention of substituting for the two old stations which had long been inadequate in every way a structure commensurate with the dignity of the city," the *Sunday Star* newspaper reported on November 24, 1907. (Both, courtesy of the Library of Congress.)

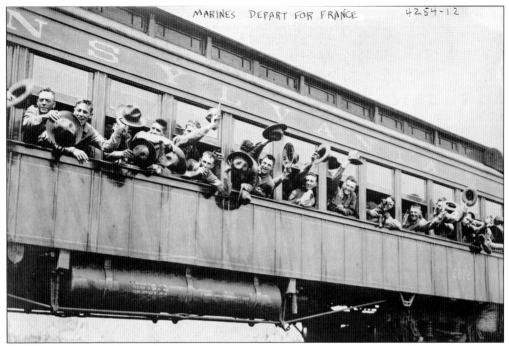

During World War I, Union Station was a popular departure point for many soldiers heading to training camp or overseas. Above, Marines prepare to depart Union Station during World War I. Below, the American Red Cross operates a canteen and mail service during the Great War. (Both, courtesy of the Library of Congress.)

Because of its location, presidents and foreign dignitaries often passed through Union Station. Above, Pres. Theodore Roosevelt appears at Union Station around 1918 or 1919, after his presidency. Below, Pres. Calvin Coolidge poses at the station in 1920 or 1921, perhaps when he was still Warren G. Harding's vice president. (Both, courtesy of the Library of Congress.)

Union Station quickly established itself as a vital transportation hub. By 1932, the station saw 285 trains every day operating over 32 tracks and carrying roughly 30,000 passengers to and from the station. However, the pace of passenger traffic waned after World War II, and by the late 1960s, the volume of travelers declined to roughly 7,000 passengers per day. The dip in volume prompted the Washington Terminal Company to consider selling the building for redevelopment. (Both, courtesy of the Library of Congress.)

"This great station forms the grand gateway to the capital, through which every one who comes to or goes from Washington must pass; as there is no railroad entering the city that will not use the station, it becomes the vestibule of the capital. This being the fact, the importance of this station is greater than that of any other one in any city in the world," the McMillan Commission wrote in its 1902 report. (Both, courtesy of the Library of Congress.)

The Union Station Redevelopment Act of 1981 said, in part, "It is in the national interest to preserve the architectural features of Union Station and to provide in the Union Station complex a sound and fully operational transportation terminal." Pres. Ronald Reagan signed the act into law on December 29, 1981. "This legislation will help to turn the Union Station complex into a successful commercial center with access to several modes of transportation," Reagan said in a statement on signing the act. (Both, courtesy of the Library of Congress.)

Following a roughly $160 million restoration project, the current iteration of the station opened on September 29, 1988. "It was a masterpiece, and it is a masterpiece," the *Philadelphia Inquirer* quoted US senator Alan K. Simpson as saying. "This place is like a fine painting we've turned over to a very careful conservator." (Both, courtesy of the Library of Congress.)

In 1987, Amtrak introduced nonstop *Metroliner* service between Washington and New York City. In 1989, after moving into the restored Washington Union Station, revenue on Northeast Corridor trains increased by more than 15 percent. That year, for the second year in a row, Amtrak carried more passengers between Washington and New York City than all airlines combined. (Both, courtesy of the Library of Congress.)

Seven

ELECTRIFYING THE LINE

As the country endured the Great Depression in the 1930s, the Pennsylvania Railroad worked to improve its main line into New York City.

On November 1, 1928, less than a year before the stock market crash that signaled the start of the Great Depression, William W. Atterbury, president of the Pennsylvania Railroad, announced a bold plan. He wanted to eliminate steam power and electrify a 325-mile stretch of line, covering 1,300 total miles of track between New York City and Wilmington, Delaware. The railroad estimated the project would cost $100 million and take upwards of eight years to complete.

The idea of electric trains was not a new one for the Pennsylvania Railroad, which used electricity to power its trains into New York City, and the railroad had already electrified a portion of its lines between Sunnyside Yard in Queens and Newark, New Jersey.

By 1931, electric locomotives were pulling trains between Wilmington and Trenton. In December 1932, the first electric train, consisting of 13 cars and carrying about 75 commuters, departed New Brunswick for Jersey City. Even as the service began, the railroad continued work on electrifying the line between New Brunswick and Trenton.

In January 1933, the first electric train to operate from New York City to Philadelphia departed Pennsylvania Station with engineer George S. Gould at the controls of the locomotive, pulling train No. 207.

In 1934, after successfully electrifying the line between New York City and Wilmington, Atterbury announced a massive project that would employ at least 25,000 workers to electrify the line between Wilmington and Washington. The Federal Public Works Administration backed the project with a $77 million self-liquidating grant. According to the January 31, 1934, edition of the *Daily Home News,* Atterbury called it "the largest corporate construction job in the country and the most extensive single program of railroad improvement undertaken in many years."

Concurrently, the railroad updated several stations along the route. Most notably, in March 1935, the new Newark Penn Station replaced a station built around 1891.

William Wallace Atterbury, pictured here in 1915, began his career with the Pennsylvania Railroad in 1886 and served as a brigadier general during World War I. In 1925, "the Railroad General" succeeded Samuel Rea as president of the Pennsylvania Railroad, serving in the post until he retired because of poor health in 1935. (Courtesy of the Library of Congress.)

The Pennsylvania Railroad dedicated its new station in Newark on March 23, 1935, a day before the station entered service. The prominent architectural firm McKim, Mead & White designed the station, opting to incorporate a mix of Art Deco and Neoclassical elements. The firm also designed Penn Station in New York. (Both, courtesy of the Library of Congress.)

The centerpiece of the electric era was the GG-1 locomotive, which operated between New York City and Washington. The Pennsylvania Railroad placed the first GG-1 locomotive into service in 1935. "Grace and symmetry will mark every line of the new engines," the *Evening Sun* newspaper of Baltimore quoted the Pennsylvania Railroad as saying in a statement. "Each end of the locomotive will slope gently inward from the floor to the cab roof, with rounded shoulders running toward the central operating compartment." (Both, courtesy of Victor Hand Collection, Center for Railroad Photography and Art.)

The Pennsylvania Railroad operated the first electric train between Philadelphia and Washington on January 28, 1935, ushering in a new era on the Northeast Corridor. The train topped 102 miles per hour, setting a new record for the Philadelphia-to-Washington run. (Courtesy of Victor Hand Collection, Center for Railroad Photography and Art.)

With the completion of electrification along the Northeast Corridor between Washington and New York City, the GG-1 locomotive became a mainstay of the Northeast Corridor for the better part of five decades. (Courtesy of Victor Hand Collection, Center for Railroad Photography and Art.)

"The Pennsylvania railroad tunnel under the Hudson river to New York city will make easy transit from New York city to Metuchen and will bring this community within one-half hour's time of the heart of New York city," the *Metuchen Recorder* newspaper wrote on April 22, 1905. "The result of this movement will be to bring a large and rapidly increasing population into Metuchen and vicinity, because it is true that Metuchen and vicinity is a very desirable place for suburban homes, and without question the land in this section is more favorably located than any other place between Metuchen and New York city." (Both, courtesy of Victor Hand Collection, Center for Railroad Photography and Art.)

"This electrification will far exceed in magnitude and in importance that of any other railroad in the world, in miles of track to be electrified, in volume and density of passenger and freight business handled, in size and amount of equipment required, in the number of trains affected, and in terminal operations involved," Pennsylvania Railroad president W.W. Atterbury said in 1935. (Both, courtesy of Victor Hand Collection, Center for Railroad Photography and Art.)

The Pennsylvania Railroad built its massive viaduct and bridge across the Raritan River around 1903. In the 1940s, the Pennsylvania Railroad encased the span crossing the river in concrete, fortifying the entire structure. "Concrete is being poured over the entire surface of the arches, brightening the former dull sandstone and heightening the symmetrical appearance of the span," the *Daily Home News* reported in a front-page story on March 16, 1946. (Both, courtesy of Victor Hand Collection, Center for Railroad Photography and Art.)

The area outside New York City—such as Secaucus, where these pictures were taken—remained remarkably rural in the 1960s. As early as 1962, state officials proposed a Secaucus transfer station located where the Pennsylvania crossed the Erie-Lackawanna Railroad. The plan was part of a larger vision for commuter railroads in northern New Jersey. However, it would take another four decades for the Secaucus Junction station to open on the Northeast Corridor. (Both, courtesy of Victor Hand Collection, Center for Railroad Photography and Art.)

Princeton Junction, pictured above, was a junction point for the Northeast Corridor and a spur that runs to the Princeton University campus. The shuttle that connects Princeton University and Princeton Junction is known as the "Dinky" or the "PJ&B" ("Princeton Junction and Back"). (Courtesy of Victor Hand Collection, Center for Railroad Photography and Art.)

The *Silver Comet* passenger train appears in Washington's Union Station. The train ran between New York City and Birmingham, Alabama. Several railroads handled the train, and the Pennsylvania Railroad operated the train between Washington and New York City. (Courtesy of Victor Hand Collection, Center for Railroad Photography and Art.)

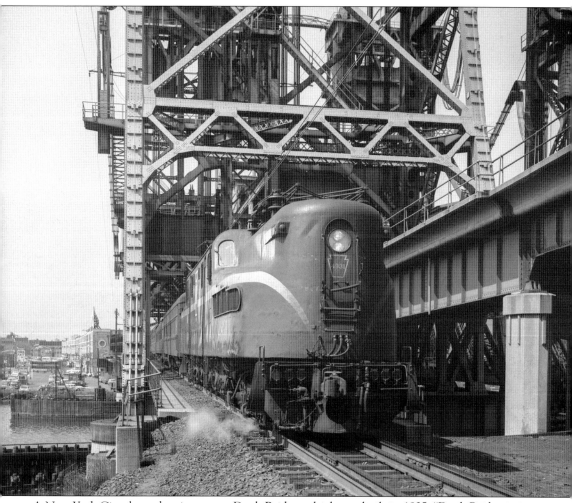

A New York City–bound train crosses Dock Bridge, which was built in 1935. "Dock Bridge is an exceptionally important Pennsylvania Railroad engineering accomplishment," according to a National Register of Historic Places inventory nomination form. "This lift bridge is an unusual engineering design in terms of its massiveness and double bridge lifts which operate independently." (Courtesy of Victor Hand Collection, Center for Railroad Photography and Art.)

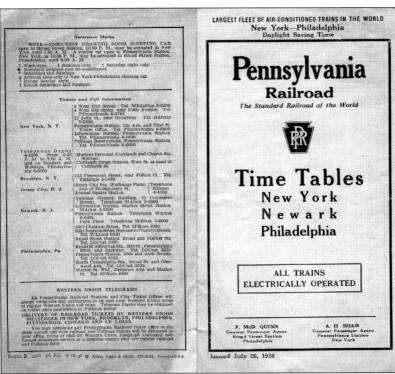

A 1936 Pennsylvania Railroad timetable touts the railroad's electrically operated trains. The timetable also notes the railroad has the largest fleet of air-conditioned trains in the world. Trains regularly departed New York City for Philadelphia, and vice versa, all hours of the day. (Both, courtesy of Railfanning.org.)

LARGEST FLEET OF AIR-CONDITIONED TRAINS IN THE WORLD

TRAINS FOR PHILADELPHIA
All Trains Daily Except as Otherwise Noted
Daylight Saving Time

TRAINS FOR NEW YORK
All Trains Daily Except as Otherwise Noted
Daylight Saving Time

New Jersey Transit continued to operate GG-1 locomotives into the 1980s, with the agency retiring its last one in 1983. "The GG-1s have a rich heritage of railroading in New Jersey and the Northeastern United States, and while all of us are somewhat saddened by their retirement, we no longer can use these famed locomotives because they are too costly to operate and maintain," the *Asbury Park Press* quoted John P. Sheridan Jr., New Jersey's transportation commissioner, as saying. (Both, courtesy of Victor Hand Collection, Center for Railroad Photography and Art.)

After years of dominating service, the 1960s was a time of trouble for the Pennsylvania Railroad. As early as 1957, the Pennsylvania began merger talks with its longtime competitor, the New York Central. The merger finally happened in 1968, forming the Penn Central; this closed the book on the storied history of the Pennsylvania Railroad and ushered in a new era for the Northeast Corridor. (Both, courtesy of Victor Hand Collection, Center for Railroad Photography and Art.)

Eight

YEARS OF TRANSITION

In 1968, the Pennsylvania and the New York Central merged to create the Penn Central, marking a new era for the Northeast Corridor. While the Penn Central was far from a financial success, in 1969 the railroad launched the innovative *Metroliner* train, a high-speed passenger train running between New York City and Washington.

The Penn Central, which also included the New York, New Haven & Hartford Railroad, was plagued from the start. At one point, the Penn Central's losses totaled $1 million per day. The company declared bankruptcy in 1970. That same year, Congress passed the Rail Passenger Service Act of 1970, creating the National Railroad Passenger Corporation, better known as Amtrak, to assume intercity passenger service from railroads.

Conrail emerged out of legislation Congress passed in the mid-1970s, including the Regional Rail Reorganization Act (the 3R Act) and the Railroad Revitalization and Regulatory Reform Act (often called the 4R Act). Conrail, which began operations in 1976, consolidated freight railroads in the Northeast and sought to make them profitable. With the action was a provision allowing Amtrak to buy the Northeast Corridor, excluding sections in New York, Connecticut, and Massachusetts that were previously sold. It also gave Amtrak a 50-percent ownership in the Washington Union Terminal Company, which owned Washington's Union Station.

Meanwhile, Conrail inherited commuter rail operations of its predecessor railroads. In 1981, Congress passed the Northeast Rail Service Act (NERSA), which freed Conrail from the obligation to operate commuter railroads.

Starting in 1983, several commuter lines began operating over portions of the Northeast Corridor, including Metro-North Railroad in New York and Connecticut, New Jersey Transit in New Jersey, Southeastern Pennsylvania Transportation Authority (SEPTA) Regional Rail in the Philadelphia region, and Maryland Area Regional Commuter (MARC) in the Baltimore-Washington area. Conrail previously transferred operations of MBTA Commuter Rail in the Boston region to the Boston & Maine.

Even after divesting its commuter operation, Conrail continued as a freight railroad for more than two decades. In the late 1990s, two private railroads, CSX Transportation and Norfolk Southern, purchased Conrail and split the company into their private operations.

Penn Central inaugurated the new *Metroliner* service in January 1969, and the train made the trip between New York and Washington in roughly three hours, about an hour shorter than previously scheduled trains. The *Metroliners* date to 1966 when the Pennsylvania Railroad ordered 61 cars from the Budd Company. (Courtesy of Victor Hand Collection, Center for Railroad Photography and Art.)

The *Metroliner* order was part of a collaborative initiative with the federal government aimed at improving rail service between New York and Washington. "There can be no doubt that service of this type is needed and must be provided," the *Daily Home News* quoted Stuart T. Saunders, chairman of the Penn Central, as saying in January 1969. (Courtesy of the National Archives via Wikimedia Commons.)

"It is our conviction that this train will be successful, and will allow rail travel to play a new role in the transportation picture of this country," the *Daily Home News* quoted Stuart T. Saunders, chairman of the Penn Central, as saying in January 1969. (Courtesy of the National Archives via Wikimedia Commons.)

"No other means of transportation can match this schedule on a center city basis," the *Associated Press* quoted Penn Central's board chairman as saying in January 1969. By mid-1969, the trains were credited with increasing passenger traffic on the New York–to–Washington portion of the Northeast Corridor by 11 percent. (Both, courtesy of the National Archives via Wikimedia Commons.)

Metroliner service was well regarded by many riders for its amenities, including on-train telephones, carpeted coaches, and food options. US representative Edward J. Patten (Democrat, New Jersey) hailed the *Metroliner* as a potential solution to the "air and highway traffic snarl," the *Associated Press* reported in January 1969. The trains operated between Washington and New York City in just under three hours. (Above, courtesy of the Library of Congress; below, courtesy of the National Archives via Wikimedia Commons.)

In 1972, Amtrak carried 16.6 million riders, a number that increased to 21 million in 1981. By 1977, the Northeast Corridor accounted for roughly 56 percent of Amtrak's passenger volume. Above, passengers buy tickets at New York City's Penn Station in the mid-1970s, while below, passengers use their suitcases as seats while waiting for a train. (Both, courtesy of the National Archives via Wikimedia Commons.)

The Pennsylvania Railroad built the two-story Hunter Tower around 1930. Interlocking towers, such as Hunter, once played an important role in controlling the movement of trains along the Northeast Corridor and its connecting lines. Amtrak continued to use the tower until about 1997, and the structure was subsequently demolished during construction of the Hunter Connection between the Northeast Corridor and New Jersey Transit's Raritan Valley Line. (Both, courtesy the Library of Congress.)

General Electric built the E44 locomotives for the Pennsylvania Railroad, and they later passed to Penn Central and Conrail. Above, an E44 pulls a train in Perryville, Maryland, while below, a locomotive operates through Metuchen, New Jersey. Conrail eliminated its use of electric locomotives in 1981, opting to use diesel for its motive power and retiring its 66 E44 locomotives. Amtrak acquired some of the locomotives. (Above, courtesy of Victor Hand Collection, Center for Railroad Photography and Art; below, courtesy of Railfanning.org.)

Nine

THE MODERN ERA

Today, the 457-mile-long Northeast Corridor is among the heaviest traveled sections of railroad in the world. It sees high-speed, regional, and long-distance Amtrak trains, but it also hosts commuter operations up and down the line.

Long Island Rail Road, New Jersey Transit, the Maryland Area Regional Commuter, Massachusetts Bay Transportation Authority, Metro-North Railroad, Shore Line East, and the Southeastern Pennsylvania Transportation Authority all operate commuter services over the corridor.

Today, an estimated 2,200 Amtrak commuter and freight trains operate on the corridor between Washington and Boston. In the 2018 fiscal year, Amtrak customers took a combined 18.3 million trips on the Northeast Corridor.

In recent years, however, officials at the federal and local levels have turned their attention to infrastructure repairs, including upgrades to the tunnel beneath the Hudson River. In October 2012, Superstorm Sandy caused considerable damage to the tunnel, necessitating rehabilitation.

In the same vein, federal officials in July 2017 released the Northeast Corridor FUTURE Record of Decision, a planning effort that aims to improve the corridor. The plan calls for the expansion to a four-to-six-track "modernized, [and] integrated rail network" with enough capacity to accommodate the projected increase in rail service. Under the plan, the corridor would also add more than 200 miles of track capacity between Boston and Providence, Rhode Island, and between New Haven, Connecticut, and Washington.

"The NEC is North America's . . . premier passenger rail corridor and improving the infrastructure is essential to maximizing performance for all train services," Amtrak president and chief executive officer Richard Anderson said in a 2019 press release. "The improvements will offer Amtrak and commuter customers a smoother and more reliable ride."

One of the most significant upgrades, at least in terms of rolling stock, was the introduction of the Amtrak Cities Sprinter (ACS-64) locomotives, the last of which entered revenue service in 2016. "The locomotives have ushered in a new era of improved performance, efficiency and reliability that is integral to keeping the people and businesses in the northeast moving," then Amtrak president and chief executive officer Joe Boardman said in a 2016 news release.

But the history of high-speed trains along the Northeast Corridor is still being written. In August 2016, Amtrak announced a $2.45 billion "multifaceted modernization program" for the Northeast Corridor. The investment includes next-generation high-speed trainsets among other improvements.

The Arrow III electric multiple unit (EMU) cars are perhaps the most identifiable commuter cars operating on the Northeast Corridor in New Jersey. General Electric built the Arrow III cars in 1977 and 1978, and as of 2019, they remained in use on the Northeast Corridor. Above, an express train passes through Elizabeth in August 2003. Below, an New Jersey Transit train passes through New Brunswick in 2018. (Photographs by the author; both, courtesy of Railfanning.org.)

To replace its fleet of aging locomotives, in the mid-1970s Amtrak turned to the AEM-7. General Motors' Electro-Motive Division (EMD) manufactured 65 AEM-7s between 1978 and 1988, and Amtrak bought a total of 54. Railfans called the locomotives "Toasters" or "Swedish Meatballs" because of their Swedish design origins. MARC and SEPTA also used the AEM-7 for their commuter operations. (Photograph by the author; courtesy of Railfanning.org.)

A New Jersey Transit ALP-44, which looked similar to Amtrak's AEM-7, pulls into Metuchen, New Jersey, in August 2003. The transit agency procured 32 of the locomotives, built by Sweden's ASEA Brown Boveri (ABB). New Jersey Transit used the locomotives until retiring them in 2011. (Photograph by the author; courtesy of Railfanning.org.)

In the mid-1990s, Amtrak began making plans for its next-generation high-speed trains. The railroad wanted trains that could reach 150 miles per hour. In March 1999, Amtrak announced plans for a new train, the *Acela*. "*Acela* is more than just a name for Amtrak's new high-speed trains," the *Associated Press* quoted Amtrak president George Warrington as saying in a statement. "*Acela* is a brand representing a whole new way of doing business." (Both, courtesy of the Library of Congress.)

Amtrak began regular *Acela* service on December 11, 2000. "The entire nation helped build *Acela Express*—it was visionary and aspirational transportation . . . It is the sparkling gem of a national passenger rail system," said John Robert Smith, a former Amtrak board member, according to Amtrak's history blog. *Acela* trains have transported more than 42 million people since launching. (Photographs by the author; both, courtesy of Railfanning.org.)

By 2016, Amtrak placed its new Amtrak Cities Sprinter (ACS-64) locomotives in service on the Northeast Corridor. Amtrak placed a $466 million order for the locomotives in October 2010. The company ordered a total of 70 of the new locomotives, which replaced its aging fleet of locomotives. "Delivery of the final ACS-64 locomotive marks a major milestone for Amtrak as this new fleet, a multimillion dollar investment, was delivered ahead of schedule and is improving service for millions of customers in the northeast," then Amtrak president and chief executive officer Joe Boardman said in an August 2016 news release. (Photographs by the author; both, courtesy of Railfanning.org.)

New Jersey Transit placed an order for 100 Bombardier MultiLevel Coach bi-level passenger railcars in December 2002, and the agency subsequently ordered additional cars. Above, a New York City–bound New Jersey Transit train pulls into Newark Liberty International Airport Station in 2016. The station, owned by the Port Authority of New York and New Jersey, opened in October 2001. Below, a train consisting of bi-level coaches pulls into the airport station in March 2018. (Photographs by the author; both, courtesy of Railfanning.org.)

BIBLIOGRAPHY

Adams, Arthur G., and Raymond J. Baxter. *Railroad Ferries of the Hudson and Stories of a Deckhand.* New York: Fordham University Press, 1999.

Brown, Robert R. "Pioneer Locomotives of North America." *Railway and Locomotive Historical Society Bulletin*, No. 101 (1959): 7–76.

DeFeo, Todd. "Northeast Corridor." http://railfanning.org/history/nec/. 2020.

Fisher, Chas. E. "America's Most Famous Trains." *Railway and Locomotive Historical Society Bulletin*, No. 1 (1921): 19–29.

Freeman, Leslie E. "The New Jersey Railroad and Transportation Company." *Railway and Locomotive Historical Society Bulletin*, No. 88 (1953): 100–159.

Hiebert, Ray Eldon. "Ivy Lee: 'Father of Modern Public Relations.'" *Princeton University Library Chronicle*, Vol. 27, No. 2 (1966): 113–20.

history.amtrak.com/blogs

Keys, C.M. "Cassatt and His Vision." *A History of Our Time.* Garden City: Double, Page & Company, May–October 1910.

Nelligan, Tom, and Scott Hartley. *Trains of the Northeast Corridor.* New York: Quadrant, 1982.

Watkins, J. Elfreth. *The Camden and Amboy Railroad: Origin and Early History.* Washington, DC: Gedney & Roberts, 1891.

Wilson, William Bender. *History of the Pennsylvania Railroad Company.* Philadelphia: Henry T. Coates & Company, 1895.

www.pbs.org/wgbh/americanexperience/features/the-rise-and-fall-of-penn-station-construction-penn-station/

DISCOVER THOUSANDS OF LOCAL HISTORY BOOKS
FEATURING MILLIONS OF VINTAGE IMAGES

Arcadia Publishing, the leading local history publisher in the United States, is committed to making history accessible and meaningful through publishing books that celebrate and preserve the heritage of America's people and places.

Find more books like this at
www.arcadiapublishing.com

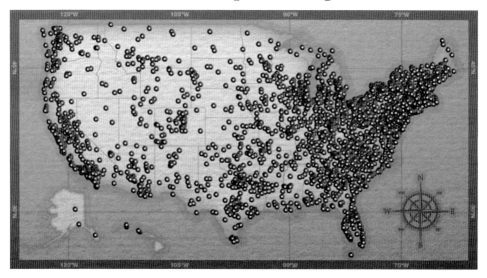

Search for your hometown history, your old stomping grounds, and even your favorite sports team.

Consistent with our mission to preserve history on a local level, this book was printed in South Carolina on American-made paper and manufactured entirely in the United States. Products carrying the accredited Forest Stewardship Council (FSC) label are printed on 100 percent FSC-certified paper.

MADE IN THE USA